Contents

Page

TABLES IV

ACKNOWLEDGEMENTS V

ABSTRACT VI

THE IMPORTANCE OF COUNTERING THE NORTH KOREA SPECIAL
    PURPOSE FORCES THREAT 1
    History 2
    Geography 5
    Weather 7
    Population 8
    Infrastructure 8
    Fielded Forces 9

NORTH KOREA'S SPECIAL PURPOSE FORCES 12
    Typical Missions 13
    A Word On Tunnels 14
    Airborne Forces 14
    Reconnaissance Brigades 15
    Light Infantry 15
    Maritime Special Purpose Forces 15
    Stealth Ships 16
    DPRK's Submarines 17
    Amphibious Light Infantry Brigades 18

COUNTERMEASURES 21
    Target Detection is the Key 21
    Mines and Anti-Ship Missiles 22
    Fixed Wing Attack Fighters 23
    AC-130 Spectre Gunships 23
    Navy Surface Combatants 24
    U.S and ROK Submarines 24

Naval Air Power 26

JOINT REAR AREA OPERATIONS 28
Homeland Reserve Forces 28
Civil Defense Corps..29
Role of the HRF and CDC in Response to Maritime Attack................................29
Base Defense 30

AH-64 APACHE ATTACK HELICOPTERS TO THE RESCUE 32
Missions...32
Destroy the Weapon's Platforms...33
Attacking the Maritime SOF Threat – A Joint Approach....................................34
Command, Control, Computers and Intelligence (C4I)..36
Battle Damage Assessment 37
Safeguards 37
Training and Equipment Issues 38

CONCLUSION..41

GLOSSARY 43

BIBLIOGRAPHY..46

Illustrations

Page

Figure 3. Aircraft Carrier laden with Army Helicopters...33

Tables

Page

Table 1. SPF Force Matrix..12

Acknowledgements

Writing an accurate account about the conflict in Korea would be an impossible task without the help of several individuals and institutions.

I wish to thank the librarians of the Air University Library, especially Mr. Chang, for their patience and willingness to assist me with my work. I would also like to thank Richard Young, a web page administrator for United States Navy amphibious units, for his assistance in finding several texts and Internet links. I would like to acknowledge Major Tim Lolatte and Major Ike Eisenhauer for their assistance in the use of the Air University research template.

Finally, I would like to thank LTC Jeffrey Reilly (former planner on the Combined Forces Korea staff) and Major Russell Stinger (former planner for deep operations on the 8th Army staff) for their insights into the continuing "Cold War" over there. Having never been to Korea, their assistance in distinguishing fanciful ideas from cold reality was helpful. Their unique insights and knowledge on the North Korean military was generous and significant.

AU/ACSC/102/1999-04

Abstract

As United States and Republic of Korea forces stand to defend against a DPRK attack, one of the most formidable tasks is how to counter a second front in the Joint Rear Security Area of the Republic of Korea.

North Korea has a robust and diverse special operations force capability, their 'Special Purpose Forces.' With nearly 104,000 soldiers committed to these daring tactics and operations, the United States and the Republic of Korea must be vigilant and innovative to protect their forces from such attacks.

The principal mission of the North Korean Special Purpose Forces is to infiltrate into the enemies rear area and conduct short duration raids. Their most dangerous avenue of approach for their forces includes amphibious approaches, airborne infiltration and the use of a vast tunnel network. How would the North carry out such an attack against such formidable foes? Will they use special operation's type forces to disrupt the South in their rear areas? How would they move their forces into South Korea? What solutions does the United States and the Republic of Korea have to solve this problem and which one is the best?

This analysis examines the various methods the United States and the Republic of Korea will use to counter the North Korean Special Purpose Forces today and in the future.

Chapter 1

The Importance of Countering The North Korea Special Purpose Forces Threat

> *...the military threat from North Korea has not subsided – here, the "Cold War" is not over, and the North's military remains formidable, unpredictable and dangerous. A significant concern is the North's SOF, designed to wage war on a "second front."*

—General John H. Tilelli Jr., Commander in Chief, Combined Forces Command

According to Joseph Bermudez, North Korea's (DPRK) Special Purpose Forces (SPF) are poised to infiltrate into South Korea and disrupt the Combined Forces Command of South Korea's rear area operations. They will attempt to destroy or capture soft targets such as Army logistics bases and Air Force bases.[1] This force is capable of massing and appearing anywhere if hostilities recommence between the two Koreas. With over 104,000 elite soldiers, these soldiers can arrive on the battlefield by hovercraft, helicopter, light planes and parachutes, tunnels, submarines, and by boat. Countermeasures such as those found in joint doctrine and/or adaptive planning may be the key to countering this threat. Historical perspective, doctrine, training and vigilance remain the tools soldiers use to counter the SPF. The SPF threat is real and only meters away, awaiting instructions to ignite hostilities and reunify the Koreas by force.

Armed Forces Staff College Publication 1, the Joint Staff Officer's Guide (1997) defines "joint" as "activities, operations, organizations, etc., in which elements of two or

1

more Military Departments participate.[2] It further defines "adaptive planning" as the concept that calls for development of a range of options, encompassing the elements of national power (diplomatic, economic, and military), during deliberate planning that can be adapted to a crisis as it develops."[3]

This paper investigates, examines and researches the historical perspectives of this threat, joint doctrine and procedures used to counter special operation's forces within the full context of the Korean conflict. I will place special emphasis on countering the Maritime Special Purpose Forces (SPF) of North Korea in order to highlight the danger this threat poses to CFC forces. Joint doctrine and adaptive planning may not be adequate to prepare our forces for this type of fight. This research will demonstrate that the best remedy to solve the threat from North Korea's Special Purpose Forces Maritime threat is the use of Army Attack Helicopters (AH-64 Apache) in an integrated approach using all assets at the CFC Commander's disposal will defeat the SPF Commandos.

This study will include research of historical lessons learned through books, journals, military monographs, and ACSC research papers and defense periodicals. I will also include the use of government publications such as field manuals, training circulars and handbooks. In addition, the research will provide information from an officer who formerly served in the Korean theatre and an Army Attack Helicopter pilot.

History

Over forty-five years after the end of the Korean War, the Democratic People's Republic of Korea (DPRK) remains at war with their neighbors to the south. Despite the end of the Cold War, the Korean peninsula maintains the highest density of military forces in the entire world, sixty-five per cent of which are within fifty kilometers of the

DMZ. It's of particular importance to the forces and people of the United States. In 1995, U.S. Army General Gary Luck, Commander of U.S. Forces in Korea, stated that if there was a full-scale war with the North, estimated casualties to Americans ranged from 80,000 to 100,000.[4] The DPRK remains committed to Korean unification by force. How would the North carry out such an attack against the South? Can the DPRK's Special Purpose forces leverage a victory for the North? This question has perplexed both United States and Republic of Korea war planners for years. A consolidated and brief analysis loosely using Warden's five ring model[5] is the best way to introduce the reader to the problems facing the Joint and Combined Forces of the Republic of Korea (ROK) by examining the history, infrastructure, population, system essentials and fielded forces of the DPRK.

Deceased President Kim Il Sung repeatedly threatened the Republic of Korea (ROK) between the end of the Korean War on July 27, 1953 and his death.[6] After his son ascended to the Presidency, the objectives of the DPRK remained the same: one Korea under Pyongyang control. DPRK policies, operations and clashes with the ROK are countless in the past forty-six years. Terrorist attacks included assassination attempts on South Korean presidents (such as the unsuccessful attempt to assassinate President Park Chung Hee where the DPRK terrorist killed his wife; and the attempt to kill President Chun Doo Hwan in Rangoon that resulted in the killings of seventeen ROK officials in 1983).[7] Three DPRK operatives that arrived in Rangoon aboard a merchant ship carried out the attack on President Hwan.[8] Another infamous incident included the bombing of a Korean Airline 747 that killed 115 passengers.

Perhaps the most daring example of the North Korean SPF capability and commitment is the Blue House Raid of 1968.[9] On 17 January, 1968, a thirty-one-man detachment from the DPRK's Special Purpose Forces (reconnaissance) breached the chain-link fence on the DMZ, donned ROK uniforms and infiltrated closer than one kilometer to the official residence of the ROK president, Park Chung Hee.[10] The daring raid was foiled when the SPF commandos captured three woodcutters and released them unharmed. The woodcutters reported the incident and although the intent of the commandos was not known, the heightened alert prevented the raid on the Blue House when a suspicious local policeman just outside the residence began to interrogate the intruders and resulted in a firefight. Although the commando team was either killed or captured, they killed seventy-one (three were Americans) people and wounded sixty-six during their attempted exfiltration back to North Korea.[11]

This threat continues today. As recently as 1995, a DPRK representative to a joint meeting in 1995 with the ROK stated that if war broke out between the two countries that "Seoul will turn into a sea of fire"[12]. Indeed, the DPRK committed over 76,000 transgressions against the armistice treaty since 1953.[13]

Any introduction to the conflict in Korea would be incomplete without a discussion

and description of the military geography of this peninsula. Its is over 600 miles long

and just over 100 miles wide at the center. It covers about the same area as Utah but is

more like the shape of Florida.[14] It shares 850 border miles with China and about

nineteen nautical miles with Russia in the northeast. The Sea of Japan abuts its eastern

coast and the Yellow Sea (as well as the Korea Bay) touches the western shores.[15] There

are few natural harbors found in either country. Pusan and Inchon are the best in the

ROK while Nampo is the best in the North with adequate harbors found in Wonsan and Chongjin.[16] The coastlines remain great distances away from densely populated areas or valuable military targets. However, the rugged shorelines are an excellent avenue of approach for small and large scale amphibious attacks.

The Demilitarized Zone (DMZ), oriented slightly northeast to southwest along the 38th Parallel, separates the two countries. It remains the de facto boundary between the two countries since the armistice. Soldiers from each country secure and patrol each respective side of the DMZ. It is about two and one-half miles wide and uninhabited. The DPRK owns just over half of the Korean Peninsula and the ROK owns the rest. Most of Korea abounds with hilly, sometimes mountainous terrain. Eastern flowing rivers flow quickly from the mountains to the sea while the western running rivers are mostly long and flow across the flood plains until they reach the long, "irregular coast that is studded with hundreds of islands."[17] On the side of the Sea of Japan, maritime approaches are clear of most obstacles while the West Coast, bounded by the Yellow Sea, is full of mud flats and islands.[18]

Weather

Korean winters are cold and windy. The temperatures can freeze the rivers, rice paddies and lakes over-night. It is just the opposite in the summer: hot and humid. The occasional typhoon rises from the Sea of Japan and with it torrential rains.[19] "Multi-layered clouds, low ceilings, winter icing, fog, and high winds make air-to-ground combat perilous among mountain peaks."[20] Korean weather remains as unforgiving and challenging as ever. DPRK military commanders may use this to their advantage should the inevitable assault by the North occur. North Korea's military commanders understand that to use their heavy forces effectively, they must avoid choke points and bottle necks in route to their objectives.[21] Will this make them wait until a deep winter freeze hits the Korean Peninsula in order to enable their heavy tanks and equipment to speed across lakes, rivers and rice paddies?[22] Fog, low cloud ceilings and precipitation tend to negate, to a degree, the effects of superior ROK and U.S. Air Forces. Despite their all-weather monikers, these aircraft will tend to have difficulty performing their Battlefield Air Interdiction (BAI) and Close Air Support (CAS) roles in these conditions although they will still be able to bomb large targets and structures.[23]

Population

The population of DPRK and the ROK has nearly tripled since 1950. At the start of the Korean War, the DPRK had 9 million people while the ROK had 21 million. Much of each country's population lives in close proximity to the DMZ. Today, the DPRK has 23 million and the ROK has 45 million people respectively.[24] Over 11 million people live in Seoul, Korea alone. The population of each of these countries has changed from an agrarian culture to a more urban one, although most people in both countries spent time on farms.[25] The largest population concentration is near Inchon in the ROK. Four other cities contain populations of over 1 million people in the ROK while Pyongyang is the only city in the DPRK that can stake that claim.[26] Other large and important cities in the DPRK include the port cities of Nampo and Wonsan.

Infrastructure

There are few paved roads in the DPRK. Some of the better ones link Pyongyang to the area vicinity of the DMZ. They are wide enough to accommodate their fighter-bombers in time of war, adjacent to their airfields.[27] They have two railways that support each coast[28]. The ROK has many railroads and an exceptional highway system linking Seoul to all other major cities and a preponderance of the countryside.[29] ROK roads, if captured, can naturally accommodate an invasion from the North

Seoul and Pyongyang are the military and governmental nerve centers of their respective countries. A loss of either city to their opponent would be a crucial loss indeed.[30] The closeness of each city to the DMZ only increases the emphasis each country places on security of these municipalities. Each country has its share of nuclear power plants, airfields and numerous military installations. Tens of millions of people reside in each city. Thousands of American citizens and military personnel reside in Seoul.

Fielded Forces

Each of the Korean forces places a high priority on their ground forces. The DPRK is numerically superior in most areas including tanks, artillery platforms and personnel. The ROK has superior numbers in armored personnel carriers, infantry fighting vehicles and helicopters.[31] "The U.S. 2d Infantry Division, deployed near the DMZ, does little to redress the imbalances"[32] quantitatively. There are roughly 36,000 U.S. troops committed to the defense of the ROK. Only the technological and training superiority of U.S. Forces will make the difference in time of war.

Neither Navy has a considerable advantage over the other. The ROK would ultimately be reliant upon a Carrier Battle Group (CVBG) to defend against the DPRK blue water forces although the ROK has a numerical advantage in surface combatants.[33] Indeed, the ROK can probably expect two CVBGs within a week of hostilities. The DPRK would rely heavily upon their torpedo boats and their expertise in operating along the Korean Peninsula's coastlines. The DPRK does not have a Marine Corps but they do have Amphibious Light Infantry.[34] The ROK has a Marine Division assigned to the defense of the country.[35]

DPRK and ROK Air Forces are roughly equal. The ROK has a slight advantage in numbers of rotary platforms or helicopters. The United States fixed wing assets and surveillance aircraft such as the Airborne Warning and Control System (AWACS) would provide the ROK with an obvious advantage.[36] It is doubtless that vastly superior U.S. Air Forces would quickly establish air superiority over the Korean peninsula with their considerable technological and training advantage. The only hope that the Korean People's Army (KPA) has to counter the South's Air Forces is to infiltrate the ROK prior to the outset of hostilities and destroy their airfields and aircraft such as those at Osan Air Force Base.[37]

U.S. Army, Navy, Air Force and Marine Corps forces are allocated and apportioned to assist in the defense of the ROK at the outset of hostilities. However, the "Pentagon's Inspector General, for example, recently found inadequate preparations for the reception, staging, and onward movement of U.S. forces scheduled to reinforce South Korea."[38] Officials inside the Department of Defense and Congress wonder out loud whether or not there would be sufficient forces to fight in Korea while simultaneously fighting in another theatre such as Iraq.[39] The bottom line is that Combined Forces Command Korea may have to fight and win with the forces on hand.

Notes

[1] Bermudez, Joseph S. Jr., North Korean Special Forces, Jane's Publishing Company, Surrey, United Kingdom, 1988, p. 2

[2] Armed Forces Staff College Publication 1, <u>The Joint Staff Officer's Guide 1997</u>, Armed Forces Staff College, Norfolk, Virginia, 1997

[3] Ibid

[4] ERRI Daily Intelligence Report, *North Korea – Preparing for War?*, Jeremy Zakis and Ronald Lewis, On-line, Internet, available from http://www.emergency.com/cntrterr.htm

[5] Warden, John A. III, *Air Theory for the 21st Century*, War Theory, Air University Press, Maxwell Air Force Base, Alabama, 1994, p. 285

[6] Congressional Research Service, CRS Issue Brief, *Korean Crisis 1994: Military Geography, Military Balance, Military Options*, No. 94-311S, 11 April 1994, John M. Collins, On-line, Internet, available from http://www.fas.org/spp/starwars/crs/94-311S.htm

[7] Ibid

[8] Ibid

[9] Bolger, Daniel P., Scenes from an Unfinished War: Low Intensity Conflict in Korea, 1966-1969, Leavenworth Papers No. 19, Combat Studies Institute, U.S. Army Command and General Staff College, Ft. Leavenworth, Kansas, p. 62

[10] Ibid, p. 63

Notes

[11] Ibid, p. 65

[12] Ibid

[13] Ibid

[14] Congressional Research Service, CRS Issue Brief, *Korean Crisis 1994: Military Geography, Military Balance, Military Options*, No. 94-311S, 11 April 1994, John M. Collins, On-line, Internet, available from http://www.fas.org/spp/starwars/crs/94-311S.htm

[15] Ibid

[16] Ibid

[17] Ibid

[18] Ibid

[19] Ibid

[20] Ibid

[21] Ibid

[22] Ibid

[23] Ibid

[24] Ibid

[25] Ibid

[26] Ibid

[27] Ibid

[28] Ibid

[29] Ibid

[30] Ibid

[31] Ibid

[32] Ibid

[33] Ibid

[34] Bermudez, p. 86

[35] Congressional Research Service, CRS Issue Brief, *Korean Crisis 1994: Military Geography, Military Balance, Military Options*, No. 94-311S, 11 April 1994, John M. Collins, On-line, Internet, available from http://www.fas.org/spp/starwars/crs/94-311S.htm

[36] Ibid

[37] Bermudez, p. 86

[38] Congressional Research Service, CRS Issue Brief, *Korean Crisis 1994: Military Geography, Military Balance, Military Options*, No. 94-311S, 11 April 1994, John M. Collins, On-line, Internet, available from http://www.fas.org/spp/starwars/crs/94-311S.htm

[39] Ibid

Chapter 2

North Korea's Special Purpose Forces

Table 1. SPF Force Matrix

Number of Units	Type of SPF Unit	Number of Soldiers
44	Light Infantry Battalions	48,200
8	Airborne Brigades	30,000
4	Reconnaissance Brigades	16,800
3	Amphibious Brigades	9000

Source: Bermudez, Joseph S., Jr. North Korean Special Forces. Jane's Publishing Company, Surrey, United Kingdom, 1988.

Special Operation's Forces are units specially trained, equipped, and organized to conduct strategic or tactical missions in pursuit of national military, political, economic or psychological objectives.[1] The Department of Defense North Korea Handbook reveals that the DPRK's Special Purpose Forces (SPF) are organized into twenty-two brigades and seven battalions.[2] This handbook also points out that these forces perform several missions including reconnaissance, disrupting rear area operations, protecting DPRK rear areas and maintaining internal security.[3] FM 100-16, *Army Operational Support*, lists security as the most important function of the four major activities to assure freedom of maneuver and continuity of operations.[4] Are we ready to counter an attack by North

Korea's Special Purpose Forces? Understanding the typical missions, organization, equipment and intentions of the SPF is the first step towards securing our forces from the SPF.

Typical Missions

"Special Operations Forces (North Korea's) were developed to meet three basic requirements: to breach the flank-less fixed defense of South Korea, to create a "second front" in the enemy's rear area, disrupting in-depth South Korean or United States reinforcements and logistical support during a conflict, and to conduct battlefield and strategic reconnaissance."[5]

On July 21, 1998, a United States spokesperson was quoted in the Kyodo Newspaper (Seoul), that U.S Naval forces would support the ROK's efforts to prevent North Korean infiltration into the ROK's territorial waters.[6] Combined Forces Command and the Naval Combatant Command were reacting to the capture of a DPRK submarine caught off of the eastern coast of South Korea the day before this announcement. Infiltration by submarine has become almost commonplace in the last twenty years either by accident (one submarine became stuck on a South Korean offshore reef) or by design.

There are countless reports of similar espionage activities by North Korea's Special Purpose Forces but the best example is the Ulchin-Samchok Landings on 30 October, 1968 when Maritime SPF commandos landed on beaches at eight different locations in the ROK.[7] The objective was to establish guerilla bases in the south to gather intelligence. An intense, coordinated response by the United States and ROK active duty and reserve forces within the Joint Rear Security area expelled the intruders (over 110 SPF soldiers killed). However, the infiltration of this one company caused the mobilization of over 70,000 men and cost the lives of sixty-three South Koreans to include twenty-three civilians.[8]

A Word On Tunnels

In addition to their distinct organizational designs and capabilities, the Special Purpose Forces take advantage of unique infiltration avenues such as tunnels. "The North Korean People's Army has formulated techniques to bring surprise and chaos to the Army of the South…one such technique is the use of underground tunnel systems that run from the north to the South beneath the Demilitarized Zone."[9]

The United States and the ROK discovered tunnels with the capacity to move over 10,000 KPA soldiers an hour to pass through to the South.[10] Although these tunnels are suited for regular KPA units, the Special Purpose Force Reconnaissance units will use these tunnels as well. It is admittedly extremely difficult for the KPA to move past the vigilant forces of the ROK and the U.S. that are located at the DMZ area but they continue to do so despite the risks.[11]

Airborne Forces

Special Purpose Forces use the antiquated but effective AN-2 Colt to infiltrate the ROK by air. This wooden plane belonging to the Korean People's Air Forces (KPAF) is difficult to detect by allied radar systems. The KPA's elite airborne forces can either air-land or parachute from the AN2 Colt to insert their paratroopers. The DPRK has over 300 of these aircraft and they can range as far south as the ROK's southernmost airfield of Cheju.[12] Only the KPA's best soldiers serve in the Airborne Light Infantry.

Reconnaissance Brigades

These reconnaissance brigades sometimes known as 'sniper' brigades are part of the ground intelligence efforts of the KPA.[13] These units have the ability to not only conduct intelligence gathering but also perform a direct action role as well. They train and equip to seize or destroy strategic targets within the ROK. Additionally, it is suspected these units carry out assassination attempts.[14] Joseph Bermudez suggests in his book <u>North Korean Special Forces</u> that airfields such as the one at Osan Air Force Base in South Korea are priority targets for the reconnaissance brigades.[15]

Light Infantry

KPA light infantry battalions are found in forward deployed and rear-area corps-level units of North Korea.[16] These units are normally battalion size and may be assigned to divisional units or formed as separate battalions. The light battalions are similar to their amphibious light infantry counterparts but do not routinely receive amphibious training. The major focus of the light infantry is the "rapid infiltration and disruption of enemy rear areas through concealed movement."[17] The missions of the light infantry include seizure of forward area lines of communication, and destruction of high-payoff targets such as nuclear or chemical sites.[18] In keeping with their name, they are lightly armed and equipped with small arms and antitank weapons.

Maritime Special Purpose Forces

"The North Korean Maritime SPF threat is very real, substantial and dangerous. The CFC must intercept and destroy infiltrating maritime SPF elements to prevent them from reaching the ROK coastline and infiltrating into the ROK interior to disrupt CFC's rear operations."[19]

As was the case with Iraqi forces during Desert Shield/Desert Storm, an amphibious threat can draw away precious assets from other areas of defense. Iraqi Forces moved over 80,000 troops along the shorelines of Kuwait in response to a possible amphibious invasion by U.S. Marines.[20] The SPF Maritime forces compel the ROK and U.S. Forces to array vast defenses in order to respond to this avenue of approach. Estimates reveal that the North Korean's can deliver over 7,000 SPF personnel to each of the ROK coastlines.[21] Based on the number of ships available to the SPF, they could deliver 5,000 of these soldiers in one lift (approximately 102 amphibious craft).[22] It is expected that these special forces once ashore, will attempt to infiltrate South Korea's rugged terrain to attack the ROK in their rear areas just before and during the renewed commencement of hostilities between the two countries.[23]

Stealth Ships

News services in South Korea report ROK Defense Ministry sources revealing the development of a North Korean Stealth Ship capable of infiltrating the ROK coasts undetected by modern surveillance and radar systems.[24] The boat is estimated to be thirty-eight meters long with radar absorbing paint and faceted surfaces.[25] It has a speed of over 50 kilometers per hour with 57mm and 30mm machine guns mounted.[26] It can ferry a team of up to thirty commandos. This report along with the report of new semi-submersibles and new mini-submarines accentuate the efforts of the North Korean's to exploit this avenue of approach and the concern that has brought to the Defense Ministry of South Korea.

DPRK's Submarines

The DPRK SPF forces can infiltrate the ROK coastlines through use of submarines. The DPRK Navy has twenty-four Romeo class diesel electric submarines of a 1950s Soviet design.[27] These submarines are used primarily in the coastal areas and an excellent platform to deposit small units offshore. Their Navy also has four or five Whiskey class coastal submarines but may only be used for training due to a shortage of parts and the age of the equipment.[28] Specially outfitted Sang-O submarines carry a small crew of nineteen and serve a sole purpose of coastal infiltration. Finally, the DPRK Navy possesses at least forty-five midget submarines ideally suited to infiltrate two to five man teams into the ROK.[29] Despite the technological advantage of the south, such small submarines prove difficult to detect especially along the rugged coastlines of the Korean Peninsula.

One Sang-O submarines ran aground a reef 120 kilometers south of the DMZ on the East Coast of the ROK in 1996.[30] A taxi driver first noticed several young men sitting beside a highway roadside, all in the same uniforms with military haircuts.[31] The taxi driver reported the incident to the police beginning a massive manhunt that resulted in the deaths of twenty of the submarine's crewmen. There are reports that SPF commandos, the cargo on the submarine, killed the submarine's crewmen.[32] Although this speaks well of the alertness of ROK's civilians to vigilantly report and pursue these KPA soldiers, it also demonstrates that the Special Purpose Forces can get past the coastal defenses of the ROK.

Amphibious Light Infantry Brigades

The KPA has three amphibious light infantry brigades with a total of thirteen battalions in their inventory.[33] The difference between Amphibious Light Infantry and regular Light Infantry units within the KPA simply rests on the formers constant training with various amphibious platforms and conduct of amphibious operations. Their primary mission is to seize critical sites along the South Korean coastlines in time of war with an emphasis on the ROK's rear areas.[34] These units are roughly comparable to U.S. Marines.

The DPRK amphibious forces can call upon over six separate classes of amphibious assault craft. These craft range in size and number from the 350 ton Hantae class utility landing craft to the speedy and light Kongbany class assault hovercraft capable of speeds over fifty miles per hour.[35] In all, there are over 370 known amphibious assault craft in the DPRK Naval inventory (this includes the 102 used by the Maritime SPF).[36] They can also use rubber rafts to infiltrate from other larger platforms. This is an excellent tactic to avoid the shore patrols of ROK Navy.[37] The rubber rafts are extremely difficult to detect by electronic sensors or even by coastal sentries, especially in bad weather.

Notes

[1] Armed Forces Staff College Publication 1, <u>The Joint Staff Officer's Guide 1997</u>, Armed Forces Staff College, Norfolk, Virginia, 1997, p. 116

[2] Handbook, <u>North Korea</u>, Defense Intelligence Agency, Washington, D.C., 1993, p. 3-119

[3] Ibid

[4] Field Manual 100-16. <u>Army Operational Support</u>. Headquarters, Department of the Army, Washington, D.C., 1995, p. 15-0

[5] Special Operations Online, North Korea Special Operation's Forces, On-line, Internet, available from http://www.specialoperations.com/north korea/

Notes

[6] Jane's Information Group, IWR Daily Update, Vol. 5, No. 138, 21 July 1998, South Korea, On-line, Internet, available from http://interweb.janes.com/iwr/iv5n13803.html

[7] Bolger, Daniel P., Scenes from an Unfinished War: Low Intensity Conflict in Korea, 1966-1969, Leavenworth Papers No. 19, Combat Studies Institute, U.S. Army Command and General Staff College, Ft. Leavenworth, Kansas, p. 86

[8] Ibid, p. 87

[9] Reece, Allen D. "A Historical Analysis of Tunnel Warfare and the Contemporary Perspective." School of Advanced Military Studies, United States Army Command and General Staff College, Fort Leavenworth, Kansas, 1997, p. 20

[10] Ibid

[11] Air University, Interview with LTC Jeffrey Reilly, Air University, Maxwell Air Force Base, Alabama, 1999

[12] Bermudez, Joseph S. Jr., North Korean Special Forces, Jane's Publishing Company, Surrey, United Kingdom, 1988, p. 103

[13] Ibid, p. 125

[14] Ibid, p. 126

[15] Ibid, p. 127

[16] Ibid, p. 77

[17] Ibid, pg. 77

[18] Ibid, pg. 78

[19] Military Review, *Solving Threat SOF Challenges*, MarApr 98, General John H. Tilelli Jr., US Army, and Lieutenant Colonel William P. Gerhardt, US Army, On-Line, Internet, available from http://www.cgsc.army.mil/MILREV/English/MarApr98/tilelli.htm

[20] Proceedings, *Marine Amphibious Force Operations in the Persian Gulf War*, 2LT Michael Russ, US Marine Corps, July 1997, On-line, Internet, available from http://www.jpsnet/bpuuna/gator.htm

[21] Military Review, *Solving Threat SOF Challenges*, MarApr 98, General John H. Tilelli Jr., US Army, and Lieutenant Colonel William P. Gerhardt, US Army, On-Line, Internet, available from http://www.cgsc.army.mil/MILREV/English/MarApr98/tilelli.htm

[22] Bermudez, p. 95

[23] Ibid

[24] Digital ChosunIlbo, *North Korea Develops Stealth Ship*, On-line, Internet, available from http://www.chosun.com/w2Idata/html/news/199812/199812200240.html

[25] Ibid

[26] Ibid

[27] Bermudez, p. 84

[28] USS Salem, Fleet List: North Korean Navy, Maintained by Andrew Toppan, On-line, Internet, available from, http://www.uss-salem.org/worldnav/asrapac/n_korea.htm

[29] Ibid

[30] Time International Magazine, *Mission on the Rocks*, Nelan, Bruce W., September 30, 1996, On-line, Internet, available from

Notes

http://cgji.pathfinder.com/time/magazine/archive/1998/dom960930/koreas.html

[31] Ibid

[32] Ibid

[33] Bermudez, pg. 86

[34] Ibid

[35] USS Salem, Fleet List: North Korean Navy, Maintained by Andrew Toppan, On-line, Internet, available from, http://www.uss-salem.org/worldnav/asrapac/n_korea.htm

[36] Ibid

[37] Bermudez, p. 87

Chapter 3

Countermeasures

Target Detection is the Key

Detecting and destroying the Amphibious Light Infantry is the key to denying the

DPRK's ability to create a second front in South Korea. With this in mind, the Naval

Component Command (NCC) in Korea will use a combination of detection platforms to

detect, target, interdict, and destroy incoming amphibious forces. The NCC will attempt

to detect any amphibious force entering their area of responsibility using Antisubmarine

Warfare (ASW) helicopters (such as the Light Airborne Multipurpose Systems (LAMPs)

Mark III; Sea Helicopter 60s (SH-60); P3 Orion long-range antisubmarine patrol aircraft

shore-based radar systems; Electronic Intelligence (ELINT) from satellites; ES-3 carrier

based aircraft; and the EP-3 Signal Intelligence (SIGINT) aircraft).[1] All of these

platforms form an almost seamless defense against undetected intrusion by amphibious

forces.

Also used in the detection fight are the SH-60B and SH-60F Helicopters carried

by most U.S. Navy surface combatants.[2] Their medium-range radar as well as infrared

and electronic surveillance systems provide another capability to cover the area of

concern[3]. These helicopters have a distinct advantage over their Army Attack Helicopter

counterparts in regard to how they are vectored to a target. The data that they receive from either their host ships, AWACs, Hawkeyes or other control platforms arrives via a secure data-link. The Army's AH-64 Apache must receive their information via secure *voice* communications.[4]

The ROK adds their brown-water navy patrol craft and frigates to this fight.[5] The NCC and the ROK can use their own submarines for the detection and tracking efforts as well as E-8C Joint Surveillance Target Attack Radar Systems (Joint STARS); other airborne radar platforms such as the E-3 Aerial Warning and Control System (AWACS); and the carrier-based E-2 Hawkeye. Even the use of the ROKs Homeland Reserve Forces occupying sentry positions along the coasts can be called upon. The importance of detecting Maritime SPF units over water before they land is reinforced by the sale of technical data and assistance for the development and deployment of a littoral water surveillance system in February of 1998.[6]

Mines and Anti-Ship Missiles

"At the inception of Operation Desert Storm, it was unlikely that amphibious operations would take place, because of the minefields that lay along the Kuwaiti and Iraqi coast, and the threat posed by Iraqi anti-ship missile capabilities."[7]

Although the array of Maritime SPF forces placed against the ROK remains significant, mines can play a crucial role in deterring these commandos. During Operation Desert Storm, there was a plan to raid the island of Faylaka in the Persian Gulf in order to destroy a command post and its infrastructure. These plans were set aside when on 18 February 1991, the Landing Platform Ship (LPH10) Tripoli and the Cruiser Guided Ship (CG-59) Princeton struck mines in the coastal areas.[8] Sea mines, since their creation, remain a "major obstacle preventing naval forces from shaping and dominating the battle-space, projecting power from the sea and sustaining joint operations ashore."[9]

Fixed Wing Attack Fighters

The answer to the Maritime SPF threat may be the use of fixed-wing fighter aircraft in a sea-interdiction role. Fighters such as the F-14, F-15, F-16 and F-18 have excellent systems to fix and destroy surface combatants. But the issue, again, is one of timing. The initiation of full-scale hostilities by the DPRK will realistically force the NCC to deploy its fighter aircraft into a defense of the fleet role. Land-based fighters will need to fight to obtain air superiority over land and interdict ground targets.[10] Although these two missions will only last a day or two by most estimates, this is the perfect time for the Maritime SPF to infiltrate the ROK coasts.

AC-130 Spectre Gunships

The AC-130 Spectre Gunship has the detection devices and weapon systems to engage and destroy the Maritime SPF of the KPA. With its state of the art 105mm cannon and 40mm chain gun, the small amphibious craft would be easy targets. This asset belongs to the Special Operation's Command Korea (SOCKOR). However, the sluggish AC-130 is rarely put into the fight unless there is a low risk of attack by ground air defenses and enemy aircraft. Its is also to reasonably assume that the KPA has SA-16 shoulder fired ground to air missiles such as the American "Stinger" missile.[11] An AC-130 would be an easy target for such a weapon system. An AC-130 was shot down during the Persian Gulf War during daylight conditions in support of ground forces. It is doubtful that the

Combined Forces Commander would release this finite asset for this mission unless he had complete air supremacy.

Navy Surface Combatants

The United States Navy's 7th Fleet commander is the Naval Component Commander for Korea. This four-star Admiral is also in charge of interdicting North Korean Naval forces.[12] While the American Navy enjoys almost worldwide dominance of blue water or deep ocean areas, the brown-water areas or those areas between the coastline and about twelve miles offshore, represent a unique concern. Navigation and shallow water avoidance is difficult. Land based systems can engage your ship. This is the area that the North intends to penetrate.[13] The key to defeating these forces is detection and the ability to vector a system to kill the target once found. How can ROK forces detect such small targets as rubber rafts and hovercraft?

The ROK brings a brown-water navy to the table to counter the Maritime SPF. They are ideally suited for the role from the perspective that the SPF amphibious forces will likely hug the littorals and coast lines of the ROK to avoid the might of U.S. blue water forces. The ROK Navy consists of small frigates, patrol boats and coastal submarines although a small aircraft carrier is to be commissioned in the year 2012.[14] Shore patrols from small islands on the South Korea maintain a vigilant watch not only for amphibious craft but also for hovercraft, disguised ships, semi-submersibles, and submarines.

U.S and ROK Submarines

Confronting the North Korean submarine threat and thus countering the Maritime SPF commandos that may be aboard, provides a special problem for the NCC. Since the fall of the Soviet Union, Russia has sold submarine technology and even actual submarines for cash.[15] There is no open-source evidence that such technology or submarines have been sold to North Korea but it remains an open question. How will our Naval forces counter this lesser but lethal threat from infiltrating the coastlines of the ROK?

Submarine tracking remains centered on acoustical methods.[16] Sound Navigation Ranging (SONAR) "works on the principle of sound transmitted through water."[17] In short, SONAR relies upon listening for noise whether that noise is reflected off of the target by the listening platform or generated unilaterally by the target.[18] South Korean forces use multiple platforms to detect submarines using SONAR technology.

Anti-Submarine Warfare forces will defend-in-depth against the coastal submarines of the ROK. Countering these platforms relies on the same principle as countering the amphibious craft: track and destroy the submarines before they can deliver their cargo of commandos. To do this, the NCC will rely on P-3 patrol aircraft, Captor (encapsulated torpedo mines) and attack submarines.[19] However, the problem with these effective methods of countering the Maritime SPF threat is that these systems work in defense of Navy ship formations such as our own Amphibious Ready Groups (ARGs) and Aircraft Carrier Battle Groups (CVBGs). Will the Navy have enough assets to deal with a multi-layered Maritime SPF force alone? This is a particularly difficult question to answer when it comes to submarines. Surface forces such as fixed wing fighters and attack helicopters can only kill a submarine when it surfaces, unless the platforms is specially outfitted with a torpedo.

All of the systems available to the NCC to counter the submarine threat will not be explored in this paper. The NCCs vast array of capabilities seem well suited to countering the submarine threat, however, the NCC cannot be satisfied with those efforts given the number of small submarines that intermittently pass through his defense-in-depth either by accident or design. The NCC may have an answer to the surface ship problem but given the actual cases of submarine infiltration in recent years, the NCC still has a challenge to his coastal defense.

Naval Air Power

The NCC's Anti-surface Ship Warfare (ASUW) Commander will coordinate these tracking and surveillance efforts and direct surface ships, submarines or aircraft to destroy the enemy as required. Attack 6 (A6) aircraft, P-3 Patrol Aircraft, submarines and most surface combatants,' carry the ship-killing Harpoon missile and can respond quickly and destroy identified targets.[20] Plans are under way to fit the carrier-based S-3 Patrol Aircraft, F/A-18 Strike-Fighters and even B-52 Bombers with the Harpoon Missile, adding to the depth of platforms able to kill these targets.[21] SH-60B and SH-60F Helicopters may be able to fire the anti-ship Penguin missile in the future.[22] The Penguin missile is effective against small targets such as those used by the DPRK's Maritime SPF units. Many Navy ASW helicopters now have use of the fire-and-forget Hellfire Missiles such as those used on an AH-64 Apache Attack Helicopter. However, "the NCC simply does not have enough resources to detect, track and destroy every enemy surface vessel, submarine and aircraft in both the "blue water' and the littoral."[23]

Notes

[1] Naval Advisory Group, Employment of Navy and Marine Forces, Air University Press, Maxwell Air Force Base, Alabama, 1994, p. 47

Notes

[2] Ibid, p. 49

[3] Ibid

[4] Air University, Interview with Major Russell Stinger, Air University, Maxwell Air Force Base, Alabama, 1999

[5] Air University, Interview with LTC Jeffrey Reilly, Air University, Maxwell Air Force Base, Alabama, 1999

[6] USS Salem, Fleet List: North Korean Navy, Maintained by Andrew Toppan, On-line, Internet, available from, http://www.uss-salem.org/worldnav/asrapac/n_korea.htm

[7] Proceedings, *Marine Amphibious Force Operations in the Persian Gulf War*, 2LT Michael Russ, US Marine Corps, July 1997, On-line, Internet, available from http://www.jpsnet/bpuuna/gator.htm

[8] Ibid

[9] Ibid

[10] Military Review, *Solving Threat SOF Challenges*, MarApr 98, General John H. Tilelli Jr., US Army, and Lieutenant Colonel William P. Gerhardt, US Army, On-Line, Internet, available from http://www.cgsc.army.mil/MILREV/English/MarApr98/tilelli.htm

[11] Air University, Interview with LTC Jeffrey Reilly, Air University, Maxwell Air Force Base, Alabama, 1999

[12] Military Review, *Solving Threat SOF Challenges*, MarApr 98, General John H. Tilelli Jr., US Army, and Lieutenant Colonel William P. Gerhardt, US Army, On-Line, Internet, available from http://www.cgsc.army.mil/MILREV/English/MarApr98/tilelli.htm

[13] Ibid

[14] USS Salem, Fleet List: North Korean Navy, Maintained by Andrew Toppan, On-line, Internet, available from, http://www.uss-salem.org/worldnav/asrapac/n_korea.htm

[15] Naval Advisory Group, Employment of Navy and Marine Forces, p. 38

[16] Ibid

[17] Ibid

[18] Ibid

[19] Ibid, p. 48

[20] Ibid, p. 46

[21] Ibid

[22] Ibid

[23] Military Review, *Solving Threat SOF Challenges*, MarApr 98, General John H. Tilelli Jr., US Army, and Lieutenant Colonel William P. Gerhardt, US Army, On-Line, Internet, available from http://www.cgsc.army.mil/MILREV/English/MarApr98/tilelli.htm

Chapter 4

Joint Rear Area Operations

"A joint rear area (JRA) is a specific land area within a joint force commander's operational area designated to facilitate protection and operation of installations and forces supporting the joint force"

---Joint Tactics, Techniques, and Procedures for Base Defense, JP 3-10.1

Securing rear operations from special operation force attacks requires doctrine, training and preparation. Rear operations at the operational level of war include major logistical centers (fuel, ammo, water, parts), Air Force base operations, cities and naval ports. These 'soft' targets are often the last priority for assigning front-line Army units, Air Force aircraft or friendly Special Operation's units. The theatre level units must use their own troops, ROK troops non-withstanding, to protect against the SPF in Korea. Sound security plans, quality training, and understanding the nature of the threat will adequately prepare our forces.

Homeland Reserve Forces

The Homeland Reserve Forces (HRF) of the ROK are charged with the defense of country in time of attack by the DPRK. Formed in April of 1968, these reserve forces are subject to the command of the regular army and their training and education is provided by regular army officer and non-commissioned officer. They receive over sixty hours of training a year.[1] These forces, part-time soldiers such as those of the United State's National Guard, play a critical Counter-SPF role. Infiltrators that do pass though ROK front-line defenses are ruthlessly hunted down by the HRF.

Civil Defense Corps

Organizations of the Civil Defense Corps (CDC) exist in every community throughout the ROK. These forces are legally viable via the Basic Law on Civil Defense passed in July of 1975.[2] All male ROK citizens between the age of 20 and 50 years old and must be a member of the HRF or a member of the CDC. The local CDC elements protect lives and property in time of enemy attack and also respond to other natural or man-made disasters. There are over five million members.[3] These forces are essentially analogous to the Individual Ready Reserve in the United States. They augment the HRF forces in times of crisis.

Role of the HRF and CDC in Response to Maritime Attack

The role of the HRF and CDC in response to an amphibious landing by the KPA would be to provide sentries to guard the coastlines and augment municipal and active forces in hunting down infiltrators. They would also assist in the protection of critical sites to the ROK by patrolling local critical sites and manning checkpoints. Although these two organizations provide assistance to the ROK in time of war, they are not synchronized with United States forces assigned rear area security missions.[4]

Base Defense

"A North Korean defector said on Tuesday that the regime in Pyongyang believes that the U.S. would abandon the Korean Peninsula in less than a month if an attack on the south could inflict at least 20,000 casualties."

--Steve Macko, ERRI Risk Analyst

During testimony to the ROK Congress, the DPRK defector Choi Joo Hwai, a former Colonel in the Korean People's Army, stated that when the KPA attacks, they would focus on U.S. Forces in order to destroy American resolve.[5] The KPA believes this will quickly and adversely influence American public opinion and the American government will recall its forces. He went on to indicate that this was part of the reason that North was pushing extremely hard to research and develop it ballistic missile systems.[6] Central to the gravity of Colonel Hwai's testimony was his conviction that North Korea would attack U.S. Forces in Japan. This claim was partially substantiated in 1997 when the North Korean's launched a test-fire missile toward Japan that landed in the Sea of Japan.[7]

The intent of the KPA to inflict massive casualties on U.S. forces necessitates the need for secure rear area operations. Tight security is the best answer to prevent destruction of critical sites in South Korea, if the platforms that deliver the KPA cannot be destroyed beforehand. Joint Publication 3-10.1 defines a joint rear area as the "specific land area within a joint force commander's operational area designated to facilitate protection and operations of installations and forces supporting the joint forces."[8] By doctrine, security of the rear area is the responsibility of the Joint Rear Area Commander (JRAC). The JRAC must prioritize his assets in order to defend against the most likely and/or most dangerous threats to his bases. But the best plans of the JRAC will not protect all of the rear area. The best defense is a good offense: killing the enemy before the enemy reaches

the rear areas must be the goal.

Notes

[1] Iworld.net, *Tactical Concepts Related to the Defense of Korea*, On-line, Internet, available at http://www.iworld.net/Korea/politics/1186.html

[2] Ibid

[3] Ibid

[4] Air University, Interview with LTC Jeffrey Reilly, Air University, Maxwell Air Force Base, Alabama, 1999

[5] ERRI Daily Intelligence Report, More On Possible North Korean War Plans, Steve Macko, On-line, Internet, available from http://www.emergency.com/cntrterr.htm

[6] Ibid

[7] Ibid

[8] Joint Chiefs of Staff, Joint Publication 3-10.1, Joint Tactics, Techniques and Procedures for Base Defense, Department of Defense, 23 July 1996, p. vii

Chapter 5

AH-64 Apache Attack Helicopters to the Rescue

"The CFC now cross-attaches Army AH-64 Apache Attack Helicopters from its Ground Component Command (GCC) to its Naval Component Command (NCC)...the mission: to attack enemy maritime SOF assets before they reach ROK shores."

—General John H. Tilelli Jr., Commander in Chief, Combined Forces Command

Missions

Combined Force Command implemented a plan to use U.S. Army Attack Helicopter 64 Gunships (AH-64 Apaches) over the past two years. "The mission of the attack helicopter is to conduct rear, close, and deep operations; deep precision strike; and provide armed reconnaissance and security when required in day, night, and adverse weather conditions."[1] Attacking targets over-water is noticeably absent from this mission statement although use of this platform over water is not an entirely new concept. It is, however, one that Apache pilots rarely train to execute.[2] This venerable attack helicopter remains a major source of combat power to U.S. light and heavy Army divisions and achieved great success in its designed role during combat operations within Operation Desert Storm.

Figure 3. Aircraft Carrier laden with Army Helicopters

Destroy the Weapon's Platforms

Up until 1996, the ROK response to any maritime invasion by the DPRK was to deal

with the infiltration after the commandos landed. Defense of the rear areas was

ultimately left to the Joint Rear Area Commander to coordinate and implement security

operations with the forces available to him. The United States position is that such forces

in the rear of their operations would be more than a major headache. The policy should

be to destroy the platforms or support systems in North Korea before they can launch or

to intercept the SPF while they are still bound to their ships.[3]

A useful approach to deal with the Maritime SPF threat continued to be a pain in the side of American forces as late as 1996. CFC war planners' major concern was that the ROK assets brought to bear on this problem were focused on land, after the amphibious craft dropped off their precious cargo of SPF commandos.[4] The key to defeating this threat was to destroy the platform before it delivered the DPRK troops to the ROK coastlines. Ultimately, the best strategy is to destroy the platforms and supporting systems before they launch, while they are still in North Korea.

Tapping into the combat power of an Apache battalion represents a unique answer to this problem. AH-64s are clearly more suited to rigors of land combat and the associated protective terrain it provides. A typical tactic for an Apache is to hide defilade behind trees or dips in the terrain until another Apache or an observation platform such as an Observation Scout Helicopter 58 or OH-58 lases a target for the Apache to "pop up", fire its Hellfire missile, then return to cover. How would an Apache shoot and survive over the featureless and endless confines of the sea? Could this proven "tank killer" fill in the delta between NCC and GCC forces where the DPRK's Maritime SPF clearly had an advantage?

Attacking the Maritime SOF Threat – A Joint Approach

Combined Forces Command originally experimented with the cross-attachment of Apaches from the GCC to the NCC in late 1996 during a major Combined Field Training Exercise (CFTX), *Operation Foal Eagle*.[5] This effort provided "an example of the synergistic use of capabilities from more than one service and more than one nation to effectively attack and destroy elusive enemy targets."[6] Using the Apaches was a novel idea, but during this exercise it proved useful and the word from the pilots who flew the missions believed it was a successful mission.[7]

The United States Joint Doctrine Capstone and Keystone Primer (JDCKP) defines synergy as the "first element of operational art...(that) involves integrating and synchronizing operations in a manner that applies force from different dimensions to shock, disrupt and defeat opponents...arranging symmetrical and asymmetrical actions to take advantage of friendly strengths and enemy vulnerabilities and to preserve freedom of action for future operations."[8] The use of Apaches in this role seems to be a shining example of the use of synergy. CFC's use of land-based helicopters under Naval control places an available strength against an unsuspecting enemy amphibious force before they can deliver their cargo, thus preserving the CFC's freedom to conduct operations without worrying about being over-run in their rear area. But can the CFC Commander afford to send Apaches out over water during a full-scale attack from the North? What about the heavy divisions pouring across the DMZ, the natural targets for the Apache's weapon systems?

It's a matter of precision timing and balance. The JDCKP defines balance as "...the appropriate mix of forces and capabilities within the joint force as well as the nature and timing of operations conducted.[9] JFC's (Joint Force Commander's) strive to maintain friendly force balance while aggressively seeking to disrupt an enemy's balance by striking with powerful blows from unexpected directions or dimensions and pressing the fight."[10] There does seem to be a window of opportunity that permits the CFC Commander to release Apaches to the NCC. During first few hours, perhaps days of a full-scale attack by the North, use of the Apache's on land is a high-risk operation due to the DPRKs significant air defense systems and the likely limited use of their Air Forces. Until the Combined Air Forces can diminish the threat to the Apache, the Apache may have to sit on the sidelines and wait.[11] However, the Sea of Japan and the Yellow Sea do not harbor such air defenses. Putting the Apaches to work at sea may be a viable and intelligent option.

Command, Control, Computers and Intelligence (C4I)

The Apache's available to the CFC commander include three battalions of AH-64s belong to the assigned 6th Air Cavalry Regiment. An additional Apache battalion belongs to the U.S. Army's 2d Infantry Division. The CFC Commander will likely allow his division commander to maintain control of his own Apache battalion leaving the GCC with operational control of three battalions. Since Maritime SPF threaten both coastlines, a temporary commitment of one battalion to each coastline while keeping one battalion in reserve seems a prudent action with priority going to the west coast.

Joint Pub 6-0, Doctrine for Command, Control, Communications, and Computer (C4) Systems Support to Joint Operations, defines the fundamental objectives for C4 systems as produce unity of effort, exploit total force capabilities, properly position critical information, and information fusion.[12] Combined Forces Command developed a strategy that produced such a synchronized effort for use of the Apaches. The C4 plan between the NCC and the Apache's achieves these doctrinal standards.

If intelligence indicates that an attack is likely by the North, the CFC commander through his intelligence officer can surge intelligence assets to attempt to detect Maritime SPF movements. Naval, space and ground assets combine to attempt to locate these forces. If the Navy discovers amphibious targets, the NCC will use the "Navy Tactical

Data System – a digital communications system that blends US and ROK sensor outputs into an integrated common operations picture."[13] Once the NCC confirms there is amphibious activity meriting the release of the Apaches to his control, he submits this request to the CINC.[14]

If the CFC Commander approves release of the Apaches, the GCC tasks the 6th Air Cavalry Regiment to send an Apache battalion to either coast or both coasts as required.[15] The Brigade Commander will immediately communicate with the NCC and launch liaison (LNO) teams to command and control ships on either or both coasts as required.[16] The battalions remain under the GCC's Operational Control (OPCON), but the GCC places the Apache battalions under Tactical Control (TACON) of the NCC.[17] At this juncture, the CFC will release control of the Apaches if there is no prevailing ground attack that requires the Apaches to remain on land.

Battle Damage Assessment

Battle Damage Assessment (BDA) is left to the vision of the Apache pilot. It is doubtful that satellites can assist in this regard, especially if the target sinks. If available, the specially trained Navy SEALS could perform the mission, otherwise, the report from the pilots will be the only record. Accurate reporting of BDA will be difficult over water for the Apache pilots, particularly in bad weather or if there is an active enemy threat in the area. [18]

Safeguards

To protect the Apache while it flies from coast to sea and back, an Interrogate Friend or Foe (IFF) code is used to track the Apaches movement by NCC command and control ships.[19] The NCC assigns different altitudes to different types of aircraft, normally fencing the 200 feet level as the exclusive altitude for the AH-64s. Fixed wing fighters will fly usually above 600 feet.[20] In order to protect friendly Navy ships, once an Apache reaches a target, it must identify the target and receive authorization to fire from the Anti-Surface Warfare Commander (ASUWC).[21] This is a prudent decision give the fact that the KPA will attempt to infiltrate on a wide variety of military and civilian platforms.

Training and Equipment Issues

The are several training issues with using Apaches to attack an amphibious threat. AH-64 pilots rarely get the opportunity to do 'dunker' training.[22] This training simulates crashing in the water and taking actions to remove yourself from the cockpit while disoriented, underwater. Apache pilots do not ordinarily train with the use of emergency oxygen bottles that provide air for a crashed pilot for a few minutes while he attempts to remove himself from the cockpit.[23] Extraction training is equally important. Essentially, another Apache on scene can lower a ladder to a downed Apache and extract the pilots from the water. Again, the Apache crews rarely get the opportunity to do this important training.[24] Finally, the plan to use Apaches requires over-water gunnery techniques. These techniques require six hours a month to train to standard. Apache pilots routinely get only eleven hours of gunnery training a month due to fiscal and operational constraints.[25] Should the Apache units dedicate over half of the training hours to over-water gunnery?

Another key training requirement is learning to hover over water. Hovering over water is one of the most difficult moves for any pilot. It is easy to lose spatial orientation while firing weapon systems, because the pilot has difficulty seeing due to the smoke

38

released from rockets or the 30mm cannon.[26] The fact that the Apaches will use running fire in their attack of most Maritime SPF threats diminishes this problem to a degree.

The AH-64D Apache Longbow that is currently in the development and acquisition program phase may overcome the dependency of the current Apache on voice systems. The Apache "Longbow's digitized target acquisition system provides automated detection, location, classification, prioritization, and target hand-over…. (and) is designed to digitize and multiplex all systems."[27] This is significant when you consider the implication of, for example, an AWACs controller attempting to vector an Apache via slow and tedious voice communications to an amphibious target while trying to control countless other platforms and targets simultaneously.

Notes

[1] Department of the Army, Weapon Systems 1998, United States Army, Washington D.C., 1998

[2] Air University, Interview with Major Russell Stinger, Air University, Maxwell Air Force Base, Alabama, 1999

[3] Air University, Interview with LTC Jeffrey Reilly, Air University, Maxwell Air Force Base, Alabama, 1999

[4] Ibid

[5] Military Review, *Solving Threat SOF Challenges*, MarApr 98, General John H. Tilelli Jr., US Army, and Lieutenant Colonel William P. Gerhardt, US Army, On-Line, Internet, available from http://www.cgsc.army.mil/MILREV/English/MarApr98/tilelli.htm

[6] Ibid

[7] Air University, Interview with Major Russell Stinger, Air University, Maxwell Air Force Base, Alabama, 1999

[8] Joint Chiefs of Staff, *Joint Doctrine Capstone and Keystone Primer*, Department of Defense, 15 July 1997, p. 32

[9] Ibid

[10] Ibid

[11] Air University, Interview with LTC Jeffrey Reilly, Air University, Maxwell Air Force Base, Alabama, 1999

Notes

[12] Joint Chiefs of Staff, *Joint Publication 6-0, Doctrine for Command, Control, Communications and Computer (C4) Systems Support to Joint Operations*, Department of Defense, 30 May 1995, p.viii

[13] Military Review, *Solving Threat SOF Challenges*, MarApr 98, General John H. Tilelli Jr., US Army, and Lieutenant Colonel William P. Gerhardt, US Army, On-Line, Internet, available from http://www.cgsc.army.mil/MILREV/English/MarApr98/tilelli.htm

[14] Ibid

[15] Ibid

[16] Ibid

[17] Ibid

[18] Ibid

[19] Ibid

[20] Ibid

[21] Ibid

[22] Air University, Interview with Major Russell Stinger, Air University, Maxwell Air Force Base, Alabama, 1999

[23] Ibid

[24] Ibid

[25] Ibid

[26] Ibid

[27] Department of the Army, Weapon Systems 1998, United States Army, Washington D.C., 1998

Chapter 6

Conclusion

North Korea's Special Purpose Forces are poised to infiltrate into South Korea and disrupt the South Koreas' rear area operations. This force is capable of massing and appearing anywhere if hostilities recommence between the two Koreas. With over 104,000 highly trained and fanatical soldiers, this light infantry unit possesses the ability to inflict great harm upon ROK and U.S. forces in South Korea. The Combined Forces of Korea must prevent the infiltration of Maritime Special Purpose Forces.

Prior to 1996, the response to amphibious infiltration by Maritime SPF forces, the defense of the ROK coast, on land, was chiefly left to the HRF and the CDC in very loose coordination with United State's forces.[1] In essence, up until 1996, ROK military commanders chose to attack the infiltrators on land and not the platforms designed to deliver them. Ultimately, the mission fell to the lethal Apaches, although no single component or platform can negate the threat posed by the SPF. As trained and patriotic as the HRF and CDC may be, it was logical to pursue one platform and destroy from five to one-hundred commandos away from land rather than wait for the commandos to come ashore and then attempt to capture or kill them. The amount of resources the command would have to commit to preserve its rear area strengthens the case for killing the platforms or supporting systems offshore or in North Korea.

The Combined Forces Command appears to have a winning strategy in applying Apaches toward the Maritime SPF threat. Training, equipment and coordination shortfalls non-withstanding, it is better to defeat the threat early than have to deal with commandos in the CFC rear area. Tight base security, fixed wing fighters, the AC-130 Spectre Gunship, and the Navy can all reduce the threat posed by the Special Purpose Forces. Attacking the platforms before they land ashore or attacking their supporting systems in North Korea may provide the best solution.

The AH-64 Apache Attack Helicopter can significantly deter the SPF from infiltrating South Korea and remains the Combined Forces Command's best choice to deal with this problem. However, only a synchronized, aggressive campaign by the CFC on land, sea and air, will neutralize the Special Purpose Forces before they create a second front in the Joint Rear Security Area.

Notes

[1] Air University, Interview with LTC Jeffrey Reilly, Air University, Maxwell Air Force Base, Alabama, 1999

Glossary

ACSC	Air Command and Staff College
AH	Attack Helicopter
AO	Area of Operations
AOR	Area of Responsibility
ARG	Amphibious Ready Group
ASW	Antisubmarine Warfare
ASWC	Antisubmarine Warfare Commander
AWACS	Airborne Warning and Control System
AU	Air University
AWC	Air War College
CFC	Combined Forces Command (Republic of Korea-U.S.)
CFTX	Combined Field Training Exercise
CINC	Commander In Chief
CVBG	Aircraft Carrier Battle Group
C4I	Command, Control, Computers & Information
DOD	Department of Defense
DPRK	Democratic People's Republic of Korea (North Korea)
ELINT	Electronic Intelligence
FM	Field Manual
GCC	Ground Component Commander
JFC	Joint Force Commander
JRA	Joint Rear Area
JRAC	Joint Rear Area Commander
KPA	Korean People's Army (North Korea)
KPAF	Korean People's Air Force (North Korea)
LAMPS	Light Airborne Multipurpose Systems
MEF	Marine Expeditionary Force
NCC	Naval Component Commander
OH	Observation Helicopter
OPCON	Operational Control
ROK	Republic of Korea
SH	Sea Helicopter
SOF	Special Operation's Forces
SPF	Special Purpose Forces
TACON	Tactical Control

Adaptive planning. The concept that calls for development of a range of options, encompassing the elements of national power (diplomatic, political, economic, and military), during deliberate planning that can be adapted to a crisis as it develops. These options are referred to as Flexible Deterrent Options (FDOS). (adapted from the National Military Strategy).

Area of operations. (DOD) An operational area defined by the joint force commander for land and naval forces. Areas of operations do not typically encompass the entire operational area of the joint force commander, but should be large enough for component commanders to accomplish their missions and protect their forces.

Area of responsibility. (DOD) The geographical area associated with a combatant command within which a combatant commander has authority to plan and conduct operations. 2. In naval usage, a predefined are of enemy terrain for which supporting ships are responsible for covering by fire on known targets or targets of opportunity and by observation.

Command and control. The exercise of authority and direction by a properly designated commander over assigned and attached forces in the accomplishment of the mission. Command and control functions are performed through an arrangement of personnel, equipment, communications, facilities and procedures employed by a commander in planning, directing, coordinating, and controlling forces and operations in the accomplishment of the mission. Also called C2.

Command, control, communications, computers and intelligence. (DOD) Integrated systems of doctrine, procedures, organizational structures, personnel, equipment, facilities, and communications designed to support a commander's exercise of command and control and intelligence gathering systems across the range of military operations. Also called C4I.

Computer. An electronic machine that performs high-speed mathematical or logical calculations or that assembles, stores, correlates, or otherwise processes and prints information derived from coded data in accordance with a predetermined program.

Dunker. A mechanical device that is used to train military pilots how to survive a crash in the water.

Flexible Deterrent Options. A planning framework intended to facilitate early decision by laying out a wide range of interrelated response paths that begin with deterrent-oriented options carefully tailored to send the right signal. These options should include limited (primarily active brigade, squadron, group) military forces and preplanned requests for economic, diplomatic, and political actions appropriate to particular military actions.

Joint Rear Area. Facilitates the protection and operation of bases, installations, and forces that support combat operations.

Laser. Any of several devices that convert incident electromagnetic radiation of mixed frequencies to one or more discrete frequencies of highly amplified and coherent visible radiation.

Radar. A method of detecting distant objects and determining their position, velocity, or other characteristics by analysis of very high frequency radio waves reflected from their surfaces.

Mission. The task, together with the purpose, that clearly indicates the actin to be taken and the reason therefore. In common usage, especially when applied to lower military units, a duty assigned to an individual or unit; a task. The dispatching of one or more aircraft to accomplish one particular task.

Operational Control. (OPCON) is the authority to perform those functions of command over subordinate forces involving organizing and employing commands and forces, assigning tasks, designation objectives, and giving authoritative direction necessary to accomplish the mission OPCON includes authoritative direction over all aspects of military operations and joint training necessary to accomplish missions assigned to the command.

Special operations. (DOD) Operations conducted by specially organized, trained and equipped military and paramilitary forces to achieve military, political, economic, or psychological objectives by unconventional military means in hostile, denied, or politically sensitive areas. These operations are conducted during peacetime competition, conflict, and war, independently or in coordination with operations of conventional, non-special operations forces. Political-military considerations frequently shape special operations requiring clandestine, cover, or low visibility techniques and oversight at the national level. Special operations differ from conventional operations in degree of physical and political risk, operational techniques, mode of employment, independence from friendly support, and dependence on detailed operational intelligence and indigenous assets.

Synergy. Integrate and synchronize operations in a manner that applies force from different dimensions to shock, disrupt, and defeat opponents.

Tactical Command (TACON). TACON is the command authority over assigned or attached forces or commands or military capability made available for tasking that is limited to the detailed and usually local direction and control of movements or maneuvers necessary to accomplish assigned missions or tasks. TACON may be delegated to and exercised by commanders at any echelon at or below the level of combatant command. TACON is inherent in OPCON.

Targeting. Targeting is the process of developing and selecting targets in response to the commander's guidance, objectives commander's preparation of the battle-space and scenario and matching the appropriate weapon system to them by taking into account existing operational requirements and capabilities.

Bibliography

Air University, Interview with LTC Jeffrey Reilly, Air University, Maxwell Air Force Base, Alabama, 1999

Air University, Interview with Major Russell Stinger, Air University, Maxwell Air Force Base, Alabama, 1999

Armed Forces Staff College Publication 1, <u>The Joint Staff Officer's Guide 1997</u>, Armed Forces Staff College, Norfolk, Virginia, 1997

Bermudez, Joseph S., Jr. <u>North Korean Special Forces</u>. Jane's Publishing Company, Surrey, United Kingdom, 1988

Bolger, Daniel P., <u>Scenes from an Unfinished War: Low Intensity Conflict in Korea, 1966-1969</u>, Leavenworth Papers No. 19, Combat Studies Institute, U.S. Army Command and General Staff College, Ft. Leavenworth, Kansas

Congressional Research Service, CRS Issue Brief, *Korean Crisis 1994: Military Geography, Military Balance, Military Options*, No. 94-311S, 11 April 1994, John M. Collins, On-line, Internet, available from http://www.fas.org/spp/starwars/crs/94-311s.htm

Defense Technical Information Center, <u>Chapter 4: North Korean Military Policy and Strategy</u>, National Ground Intelligence Center, Charlottesville, Virginia, 1995

Department of the Army, Weapon Systems 1998, United States Army, Washington D.C., 1998

Digital ChosunIlbo, *North Korea Develops Stealth Ship,* On-line, Internet, available from

http://www.chosun.com/w2Idata/html/news/199812/199812200240.html

Eberstadt, Nicholas. <u>Korea Approaches Reunification.</u> M.E. Sharpe, Incorporated, Armonk, New York, 1995

ERRI Daily Intelligence Report, More On Possible North Korean War Plans, Steve Macko, On-line, Internet, available from http://www.emergency.com/cntrterr.htm

ERRI Daily Intelligence Report, *North Korea – Preparing for War?*, Jeremy Zakis and Ronald Lewis, On-line, Internet, available from http://www.emergency.com/cntrterr.htm

Field Manual 100-16. <u>Army Operational Support</u>. Headquarters, Department of the Army, Washington, D.C., 1995

Handbook. <u>North Korea</u>. Defense Intelligence Agency, Washington, D.C., 1993

Jane's Information Group, IWR Daily Update, Vol. 5, No. 138, 21 July 1998, South Korea, On-line, Internet, available from http://interweb.janes.com/iwr/iv5n13803.htm

Joint Chiefs of Staff, *Joint Publication 3-10.1, Joint Tactics, Techniques and Procedures for Base Defense*, Department of Defense, 23 July 1996

Joint Chiefs of Staff, *Joint Publication 6-0, Doctrine for Command, Control,*

Communications and Computer (C4) Systems Support to Joint Operations, Department of Defense, 30 May 1995

Joint Chiefs of Staff, *Joint Doctrine Capstone and Keystone Primer*, Department of Defense, 15 July 1997

Kimsoft.com, *North Korea Spy Operations*, On-line, Internet, available from http://www.kimsoft.com/korea/eyewit9d.htm

Kirkbride, Wayne A. North Korea's Undeclared War; 1953 -. Hollym International Corporation, Elizabeth, New Jersey, 1994

Korea Herald, *Pyongyang's Double-faced Behavior Mixed with Propaganda Activities*, On-line, Internet, available from http://koreaherald.co.kr/nkweek/wk112698/top1126.html

Iworld.net, *Tactical Concepts Related to the Defense of Korea*, On-line, Internet, available from http://www.iworld.net/Korea/politics/1186.html

Military Review, *Solving Threat SOF Challenges*, MarApr 98, General John H. Tilelli Jr.,

US Army, and Lieutenant Colonel William P. Gerhardt, US Army, On-Line, Internet, available from http://www-cgsc.army.mil/MILREV/English/MarApr98/tilelli.htm

Naval Advisory Group, Employment of Navy and Marine Forces, Air University Press, Maxwell Air Force Base, Alabama, 1994

Proceedings, *Marine Amphibious Force Operations in the Persian Gulf War*, 2LT Michael Russ, US Marine Corps, July 1997, On-line, Internet, available from http://www.jpsnet/bpuuna/gator.htm

Reece, Allen D. "A Historical Analysis of Tunnel Warfare and the Contemporary Perspective." School of Advanced Military Studies, United States Army Command and General Staff College, Fort Leavenworth, Kansas, 1997

Special Operations Online, North Korea Special Operation's Forces, On-line, Internet, available from http://www.specialoperations.com/north korea/

Special Operations Online, South Korea Special Operation's Forces, On-line, Internet, available from http://www.specialoperations.com/south korea/

Taylor, William J., Jr., and Mazarr, Michael J. "North Korea and the Gulf War: Pyongyang's "Lessons Learned." Center for Strategic and International Studies, Washington, D.C., 1994

Time International Magazine, *Mission on the Rocks*, Nelan, Bruce W., September 30, 1996, On-line, Internet, available from http://cgji.pathfinder.com/time/magazine/archive/1998/dom960930/koreas.html

Training Circular. Special Forces Operational Techniques. Headquarters, Department of the Army, Washington, D.C., 1988.

USS Salem, Fleet List: North Korean Navy, Maintained by Andrew Toppan, On-line, Internet, available from, http://www.uss-salem.org/worldnav/asrapac/n_korea.htm

USS Salem, Fleet List: South Korean Navy, Maintained by Andrew Toppan, On-line, Internet, available from, http://www.uss-salem.or/worldnav/asrapac/s_korea.htm

Warden, John A. III, *Air Theory for the 21st Century*, War Theory, Air University Press, Maxwell Air Force Base, Alabama, 1994

www.ingramcontent.com/pod-product-compliance
Lightning Source LLC
Chambersburg PA
CBHW081752280526
45789CB00008B/2832